PASSPORT TO SUCCESS

EQUITY AND TRUSTS

Old Bailey Press

OLD BAILEY PRESS LTD
200 Greyhound Road, London W14 9RY

First published 1997

© The Old Bailey Press Ltd 1997

All Old Bailey Press publications enjoy copyright protection and the copyright belongs to The Old Bailey Press Ltd.

All rights reserved. No part of this publication may be reproduced or transmitted in any form or by any means, electronic, mechanical, photocopying, recording or otherwise, or stored in any retrieval system of any nature without either the written permission of the copyright holder, application for which should be made to the Old Bailey Press Ltd, or a licence permitting restricted copying in the United Kingdom issued by the Copyright Licensing Agency.

Any person who infringes the above in relation to this publication may be liable to criminal prosecution and civil claims for damages.

ISBN 1 85836 099 4

British Library Cataloguing-in-Publication.

A CIP Catalogue record for this book is available from the British Library.

Contents

Topic 1: Express Private Trusts – The Three Certainties – Trusts and Powers

Topic 2: The Formal Requirements for the Creation of a Trust – Completely and Incompletely Constituted Trusts

Topic 3: Secret Trusts and Mutual Wills

Topic 4: Implied and Resulting Trusts

Topic 5: Constructive Trusts

Topic 6: Protective Trusts and Purpose Trusts – Trustees' Powers of Maintenance and Advancement

Topic 7: Charitable Trusts

Topic 8: The Appointment, Retirement and Removal of Trustees

Topic 9: Trustee Investment

Topic 10: Variation of Trusts

Topic 11: Breach of Trust: Defences

Topic 12 Breach of Trust: Proprietary Remedies

Key to journal abbreviations:

CLJ	Cambridge Law Journal
Crim LR	Criminal Law Review
CLP	Current Legal Problems
ELR	European Law Review
FLJ	Family Law Journal
LQR	Law Quarterly Review
LS	Legal Studies
LTeach	Law Teacher Journal
MLR	Modern Law Review
NLJ	New Law Journal
PL	Public Law

TOPIC 1: Express Private Trusts – The Three Certainties – Trusts and Powers

1. **Intention/precatory words**
   a) The settlor must be shown to have intended a trust before the court will hold that one has been created. In most cases this will be a matter of looking at words used in a trust deed or a will to see if they can be construed as a trust.
   b) Precatory words are unlikely to be sufficient to establish the intention to create a trust in the majority of cases.
   Key cases:
   - *Re Adams & Kensington Vestry* (1884) 27 Ch D 394
   - *Lambe* v *Eames* (1871) 6 Ch App 597
   - *Lassence* v *Tierney* (1849) 1 Mac and Cr 551

2. **Subject matter**
   a) 'Proper'
   Certainty as to what is the trust property is essential since the trustees must know exactly what is and what is not included in the trust. A failure by them to deal with property which belongs to the trust could lead to breach of trust.
   Key cases:
   - *Palmer* v *Simmonds* (1854) 2 Drew 221
   - *Sprange* v *Barnard* (1789) 2 Bro CC 585

   b) 'Beneficial interest'
   The beneficial interest of each beneficiary must be certain so that the trustees know exactly what or how much each beneficiary will be entitled to on distribution of the trust property and prior to that, what income should be accumulated for or paid to the beneficiary.
   Key cases:
   - *Boyce* v *Boyce* (1849) 16 Sim 476

- *Re Golay's Will Trusts* [1965] 1 WLR 969

3. **Objects/beneficiaries**

   It is essential that the beneficiaries under a trust should be clearly defined or that a formula is put into the trust which enables the trustees to ascertain them. A trust in which the beneficiaries are not ascertainable is void for uncertainty of objects.

   a) **Fixed trust**

   A fixed trust is one under which the settlor has defined the beneficial interests which the beneficiaries are to receive and the trustees have no authority to alter them. The test of certainty of objects in fixed trusts is that it must be possible to draw up a complete list of all the beneficiaries, and if this is not possible it is void.

   Key cases:
   - *IRC v Broadway Cottages Trust* [1955] Ch 20
   - *Burrough v Philcox* (1840) 5 My and Cr 72

   b) **Discretionary trusts**

   A discretionary trust is one under which the trustees are given a discretion as to who shall receive income and/or capital from the trust, and in some cases what amounts, if any, they shall receive. Certainty of objects is important when the trustees can decide who among the beneficiaries shall receive benefits from the trust.

   Key cases:
   - *Re Baden (No 2)* [1973] Ch 9
   - *McPhail v Doulton* [1971] AC 424

   c) Powers

   In dealing with the problem of what test is applied in determining who are the objects of the power, a distinction has to be drawn between cases where the power is given to trustees 'as such' so that they must exercise it in a fiduciary capacity (the 'individual ascertainability' rule applies), and cases where the power is given to a person who is not in a fiduciary position in exercising it.

Key case:
- Re Gulbenkian [1970] AC 508

4. Conceptual certainty

Where a testator or settlor makes a bequest or gift on a condition using words which are too vague for a court to apply.

Key case:

- Re Tuck's Settlement [1978] Ch 49

5. Evidential certainty

Where there are evidential problems in proving that certain claimants fall within the terms of the trust.

Key case:

- Re Tuck's Settlement, above

a) Fixed trust

In the case of fixed trusts and *Burrough* v *Philcox* type trusts it is essential that all evidential uncertainty be overcome, otherwise the principle of equal division cannot be carried out. This can normally be overcome by the admission of extrinsic evidence.

Key case:

- IRC v Broadway Cottages Trust, above

b) Discretionary trusts

If the trust is a *McPhail* v *Doulton* type discretionary trust it will not be defeated by evidential uncertainty.

Key case:

- Re Baden (No 2), above

c) Powers of appointment
    - General powers: the donee of the power is not subject to any restrictions as to whom he shall exercise the power in favour of.
    - Special powers: the donee of the power is restricted to

exercising it among a class or description of persons designated by the terms of the power.

- Hybrid powers: these are powers under which the donee may appoint to anyone except a certain class or certain description of person.

  Key case:
  - *Re Hay's Settlement Trusts* [1982] 1 WLR 202

6. **Administrative unworkability**

   a) Discretionary trusts

   Where the meaning of the words used is clear but the definition of the benenficiaries is so hopelessly wide as not to form 'anything like a class' so that the trust is administratively unworkable.

   Key cases:
   - *McPhail* v *Doulton*, above
   - *Ex parte West Yorkshire Council* (1985) The Times 25 July

   b) Powers

   The trustees have a fiduciary duty to survey the whole class of potential objects and consider whether or not to appoint; albeit that after conducting such a survey they still retain their discretion as to whether or not to appoint.

   Key case:
   - *Re Hay's Settlement Trusts*, above

Sample Questions

1. Advise the potential beneficiaries in each of the following cases whether a trust has been created in their favour.

   a) A, who had a mail order business but who has now ceased trading and has been declared bankrupt, had had an oral arrangement with his bank, Banco plc, under which all moneys received by A from customers were, pending despatch of the goods, paid into a 'Customers' Pending Orders Account'. When A ceased trading money received from 500 customers remained in this account.

b) On returning from their honeymoon to a furnished home owned by B, B said to his wife, Mrs B, 'My darling, this house and its entire contents are now your sole property'.

c) C sent his son, S, a cheque for £50,000 payable to S, together with a letter stating that 'I am sending this money to you so that when your three children (now aged 10, 12 and 14) attain full age you can distribute it amongst them in such shares as you consider appropriate'.

d) D sent his niece, N, a cheque for £10,000 payable to N and an accompanying letter said: 'It is my wish that you use this money to further your non-nuclear campaign'.

2. Consider the validity of the following provisions in a will:

a) £20,000 to Alex it being my wish that he will share the money with his children;

b) £50,000 to the general secretary of the Campaign for Nuclear Disarmament to be applied for the pursuit of the campaign;

c) £100,000 to the Football Association to be applied for the relief of families suffering distress from the death or injury of a member of their family whilst attending Football Association matches;

d) £100,000 to the general secretary of the National Union of Mineworkers, the income to be applied as to one half for the relief of poverty amongst coalminers' families and as to the other half for the provision of scholarships for the highest education of coalminers' children.

3. Henry recently died and has left the following dispositions in his will:

a) My freehold property, 'The Hathertons', to my brother Fred, trusting that he will sell it and donate the larger part to the Telford Darts Association;

b) £50,000 to Rita and Sandra in full belief that they shall use such of the money as it necessary to continue my hobby of breeding Alsatian dogs, and any remainder should be divided between my old friends at the Golf Club.

Advise as to whether the above gifts are valid private trusts.

4. In 1994 Max, a wealthy businessman and owner of a firm Maxplus & Co, made a will which contained the following gifts:

   a) I leave my house, Greystones, to my trustees on trust for 21 years from the date of my death, to be maintained and used as a sports and leisure centre for the benefit of the employees of Maxplus & Co, any former employees and any relatives and dependents of such employees, and after that time to my son, Keith, absolutely.

   b) I leave £50,000 to my son, Keith, knowing that he will use a small amount of this sum for the provision of an annual prize for the best badmington player at the sports and leisure centre.

   Max died in January 1996. Advise his executors as to the validity of these gifts as private trusts.

Further Reading

- HLT Textbook Chapters 1 and 2
- Pettit *Equity and the Law of Trusts* 7th edn 1993, Chapters 3 and 5
- Hayton 'Uncertainty of Subject Matter of Trusts' (1994) 110 LQR 335
- Luxton 'Certainty of Subject Matter: A Problem Shared?' (1994) 28 LTeach 312
- Ockleton 'Share and Share Alike? Uncertainty of Subject Matter' [1994] CLJ 448

TOPIC 2: The Formal Requirements for the Creation of a Trust – Completely and Incompletely Constituted Trusts

1. **General**

    The creation of an express private trust, inter vivos, may require certain formal requirements as to the manner in which the trust is declared. This is principally for the purpose of preventing fraud. The provisions of the Statute of Frauds 1677 are now embodied in s53 Law of Property Act (LPA) 1925 insofar as they affect inter vivos trusts.

    Key case:

    - *Milroy* v *Lord* (1862) 4 De GF and J 264

2. **Declaration of trust**

    'A declaration of trust respecting any land or any interest therein must be manifested and proved by some writing signed by some person who is able to declare such trust or by his will': s53(1)(b) LPA 1925. No formal requirements are necessary for the creation of a trust of personalty as a general rule, so long as there is some evidence showing a clear intention to create a trust.

    Key case:

    - *Jones* v *Lock* (1865) 1 Ch App 25

3. **Formalities – transfer of property**

    'A disposition of an equitable interest or trust subsisting at the time of the disposition, must be in writing signed by the person disposing of the same or by his agent thereunto lawfully authorised in writing or by will': s53(1)(c) LPA 1925.

    Key cases:

    - *Re Fry* [1946] Ch 312
    - *Grey* v *IRC* [1960] AC 1
    - *Re Rose* [1952] Ch 499
    - *Vandervell* v *IRC* [1967] AC 291

- *Vandervell (No 2)* [1974] Ch 269
- *Oughtred v IRC* [1960] AC 206

4. **Status of beneficiary/volunteer**

   Consideration and the volunteer are mutually exclusive concepts. That is, a volunteer is someone who has not given good consideration, money or money's worth. If a settlement is a marriage settlement then it may be enforced by those persons who are within the marriage consideration; they stand outside the rule that 'equity will not assist a volunteer'.

   Key cases:
   - *Cannon v Hartley* [1949] Ch 213
   - *Re Plumptre's Settlement* [1910] 1 Ch 609
   - *Pullan v Koe* [1913] 1 Ch 9

5. **Exceptions to 'equity will not assist volunteer'**

   a) Trust completely constituted

   A completely constituted trust binds all persons including the settlor, except the infamous bona fide purchaser of a legal estate for value without notice. The beneficiary can therefore take all necessary steps to protect, preserve or recover trust property, irrespective of his having given consideration or not.

   Key case:
   - *Paul v Paul* (1882) 20 Ch D 742

   b) Incomplete trust

   The rule in *Strong v Bird* (1874) LR 18 Eq 315, applies where there is either:
   - an imperfect gift of real or personal property or an intention of releasing a debt;
   - the intention of giving a property or releasing the debt continues up until the donor's death;
   - the donee is appointed executor in the donor's will or administrator of the donor's estate by the court.

Key case:

- *Re Gonin* [1979] Ch 16

- Proprietary estoppel

  Where donor has encouraged the donee to expend money or act to his detriment.

  Key cases:

  - *Dillwyn* v *Llewellyn* (1862) 4 De GF & J 517
  - *Ramsden* v *Dyson* (1866) LR 1 HL 129
  - *Pascoe* v *Turner* [1979] 2 All ER 945

- Donatio mortis causa

  Where gift is conditional on the donor's death and made in contemplation of death.

  - Donor must part with dominion over property before death
  - Property must be capable of passing

  Key cases:

  - *Cain* v *Moon* [1896] 2 QB 283
  - *Sen* v *Headley* [1991] Ch 425

6. **Covenants to settle – trustees to sue?**

   At law a covenant is enforceable as it amounts to a promise under seal. But in equity the mere fact that a promise is made under seal makes no difference. The main remedy for breach of covenant at law is damages, while the main remedy in equity is specific performance.

   Key cases:

   - *Re Cook* [1965] Ch 902
   - *Re Kay* [1939] Ch 329
   - *Re Pryce* [1917] 1 Ch 234

7. Trust of the promise

The case law clearly demonstrates that a trust may have as its subject-matter a chose in action. Choses in action include the benefit of a promise.

Key case:

- *Fletcher* v *Fletcher* (1844) 4 Hare 67

Sample Questons

1. On 1 January 1995, Peter transferred, with the appropriate formalities, Greenacre to Gerald, £100,000 to Herbert, and 20,000 shares in X Ltd to Ian.

   None of the transferees gave any consideration and no words of gift were used by Peter. On 2 February, Peter declared himself trustee of his interest in Greenacre for Amy for life, remainder to Brian. On 3 March, Peter telephoned Herbert and directed him to hold the £100,000 on trust for Amy for life, remainder to Brian. On 4 April Peter met Ian and directed him to transfer the shares to Mark beneficially. On 5 May, Peter told Nick, who owed him £30,000 not to repay the £30,000 but to hold it on trust for Amy; Nick agreed to do this.

   Peter has recently died leaving all his property to the Feline and Canine Home, a registered charity.

   Amy and Brian seek your advice whether the trusts in their favour are valid. Mark seeks your advice about the 20,000 shares in X Ltd.

2. a) 'Equity will not perfect an imperfect gift.' Discuss.

   b) In 1970, Margery, on the occasion of the marriage of her daughter, Diana, to Henry, executed a settlement under which she, Margery, covenanted with the trustees of the settlement to transfer certain shares worth £100,000 to the trustees upon trust as to one half part thereof for the benefit of Diana's existing children (by another man), Thomas and Tina, and as to the other half part for the benefit of the future children of the marriage.

   Margery died last year without having transferred the shares and leaving all her estate to her son, Charles. Diana and Henry have since divorced, there being two children of the marriage, Sidney and Sara, both of whom are of full age.

Advise Thomas, Tina, Sidney and Sara as to any claims they may have.

3. a) In what circumstances, if any, may an incompletely constituted trust be enforceable?

   b) Two years ago, Smith, who was temporarily financially embarrassed, agreed with his friend, Brown, that if Brown would pay his (Smith's) debts, Smith would transfer his holding of 10,000 shares in XY Ltd to Tick and Tock upon trust for Brown for life remainder to Brown's children, Jack and Jill. Brown paid all Smith's debts and Smith completed a share transfer form in favour of Tick and Tock but omitted to deliver it to XY Ltd for registration. Smith has recently died leaving a will made three years ago under which he left 5,000 shares to Tick and Tock beneficially and the other 5,000 to his wife, Wendy.

   Advise Brown, Jack and Jill.

Further Reading

- HLT Textbook Chapters 3 and 4
- Pettit Chapters 3, 5, 6 and 10
- Green 'Grey, *Oughtred* and *Vandervell* – Contextual Reappraisal' (1984) 47 MLR 385
- Nolan 'The Triumph of Technicality' [1996] CLJ 436

TOPIC 3: Secret Trusts and Mutual Wills

Secret Trusts

1. **General**

    Section 9 Wills Act 1837 requires the will to be in writing, signed by the testator and attested by two witnesses. However, secret trusts are in some respects an exception.

    Key case:

    - *Re Spencer's Will* (1887) 3 TLR 822

    Statute:

    - Wills Act 1837, s9

2. **Fully-secret trusts**

    Before the court will declare a fully-secret trust to be valid the following must be satisfied:

    a) Time of communication – at any time during the testator's lifetime

    Key cases:

    - *Re Boyes* (1884) 26 Ch D 531
    - *Re Keen* [1937] Ch 236
    - *Wallgrave v Tebbs* (1855) 2 K and J 313

    b) Acceptance – either express or implied

    Key case:

    - *Wallgrave v Tebbs*, above

    c) Is tenancy joint or in common?

    - Tenancy-in-common: each legatee is entitled to a separate share.
    - Joint tenancy: if tenant accepts the secret trust *before* the will is made, the trust will bind both A and B. If A accepts *after* the will is made, A but not B is bound and B can take his share beneficially.

Key cases:
- *Re Stead* [1990] 1 Ch 237
- *Moss v Cooper* (1861) 1 J & H 352

d) Impact of Wills Act 1837

- Wills Act 1837, s15: witness or his spouse cannot benefit under that will

  Key case:
  - *Re Young* [1951] Ch 344

- Wills Act 1837, s25: beneficiary must survive the testator in order to benefit

  Key cases:
  - *Re Gardner (No 2)* [1923] 2 Ch 330
  - *Re Maddock* [1902] 2 Ch 220

e) Can secret trustee benefit?

- The Wills Act does not prevent a legatee and secret trustee being a beneficiary.
- Equity? see further below under half-secret trusts

  Key case:
  - *Ottaway v Norman* [1972] Ch 698

3. **Half-Secret Trusts**

Where the testator mentions the trust on the face of the will but does not state the purpose of the trust there but, instead, tells the legatee of the trust's purpose. The following conditions must be satisfied in the case of a half-secret trust.

a) Communication: trust must be communicated to the legatee before or contemporaneously with the making of the will.

Key cases:
- *Re Boyes*, above
- *Re Keen*, above
- *Blackwell v Blackwell* [1929] AC 318

b) Acceptance: either express or implied
   Key cases:
   - *Re Boyes*, above
   - *Re Keen*, above
c) Joint or in common?: see notes under Fully-Secret Trusts, above
   Key case:
   - *Re Stead*, above
d) Impact of Wills Act 1837, ss15 and 25: see notes under Fully-Secret Trusts, above
e) Can secret trustee benefit? – general rule is no because of evidential problems
   Key case:
   - *Re Rees' Will Trusts* [1950] Ch 204

4. **Nature of secret trusts: express or constructive?**
   - Fully-secret trusts: arguably constructive because they are imposed in order to prevent fraud or by equity; also arguably express trusts (ie testator's wishes are expressed)
   - Half-secret trusts: appear to be express trusts

   Key case:
   - *Ottaway* v *Norman*, above

   Statute:
   - Law of Property Act 1925, s53(1)(b) and (c)

Mutual Wills

1. **General**
   A mutual will is created where several persons, usually a husband and wife, make wills in similar terms generally in each other's favour with a gift over to a third party. However the principle applies regardless of who the ultimate beneficiary is, on the basis of an antecedent agreement which includes a term that each will not revoke without the other's consent.

Key case:

- *Re Dale (deceased)* [1993] 3 WLR 652

2. **Mutual intention necessary**

    Key case:

    - *Re Oldham* [1925] Ch 75

3. **Irrevocable**

    Revocation may give rise to an action for breach of contract against the party who has revoked. When one party has died a constructrive trust is imposed on the survivor for the benefit of those entitled under the agreement.

    Key cases:

    - *Re Cleaver* [1981] 1 WLR 939
    - *Re Hagger* [1930] 2 Ch 190

Sample Questions

1. By his will made in 1980, Paul devised all his realty to Betty 'in the sure and certain hope that she will carry out my designs relating thereto'. On 1 January 1981, Paul orally informed Betty that she was to hold the property left to her by his will upon trust for Cecil, Derek and herself in equal shares. Betty agreed. Derek died in 1982 and his will appointed Sam his executor. Paul has just died and his realty is worth £300,000.

    Advise Betty, Cecil and Sam.

2. By his will made in 1980, Tristram, who died earlier this year, after appointing Eric and Ernie to be his executors and trustees, made the following dispositions:

    a) he devised his main residence, The Oaks, to Frank absolutely;

    b) he devised his country cottage, Rose Cottage, to his sisters, Hilda and Helga in equal shares;

    c) he bequeathed £50,000 to his brother, Bertram 'in the knowledge that he will give effect to my expressed wishes';

    d) the residue to the trustees of the British Museum.

Shortly after executing his will, Tristram orally informed Frank that he wished Frank to hold The Oaks for the benefit of his secretary's (Sonia's) children, Jack and Jill. He also wrote separately to both Hilda and Helga asking them to hold Rose Cottage for the benefit of Sonia. Hilda replied that she would do as Tristram requested but the letter to Helga went astray and Tristram's request never came to her notice.

Prior to executing his will, Tristram had handed Bertram a sealed envelope with instructions that Bertram was only to open it after Tristram's death. The letter inside the envelope expresses Tristram's wish that the £50,000 shall be paid to Sonia.

Sonia was one of the witnesses to Tristram's will.

Advise Eric and Ernie as to the distribution of Tristram's estate.

3. By his will, made in 1983, Paul left his residuary estate to Roger and Michael adding the words 'I am quite sure that they will use it for the purposes which I have communicated to either of them'. In fact Paul had written to Michael in 1982 saying that he had in mind to leave the residue to Michael and some other suitable person for 'such medical purposes as, in their absolute discretion, they should consider most desirable'. Michael had replied that though he would do his best to carry out Paul's wishes, he doubted the validity of the disposition, and Paul had replied that he would look into the matter but that if, for any reason, his purpose could not be carried out he wished Michael and his co-trustee to use the income of the property during Michael's life to assist such of their friends as they should consider most in need, with a power of appointment by will to Michael in favour of one or more of Michael's children.

Advise Michael and Roger.

Further Reading

- HLT Textbook Chapter 5 and Chapter 7, section 7.6
- Pettit Chapter 7
- Brierley 'Mutual Wills – Blackpool Illuminations: *Re Dale*' (1995) 58 MLR 95

TOPIC 4: Implied and Resulting Trusts

1. **As an interest in land**

    Implied and resulting trusts arise where a donor or settlor has made a transfer of property but that transfer does not for some reason divest him completely of his interest in the property.

    a) Express trust in conveyance

    If a couple have the foresight on acquiring property to make express declarations as to the extent of their beneficial interests in the property then these will be given effect.

    Key case:

    - *Goodman* v *Gallant* [1986] Fam 106

    b) Financial contributions/repairs and improvements/other conduct

    In cases where there is neither an express nor an acceptable informal agreement the court will look for evidence of a common intention that both parties were to have an interest in the property.

    Key cases:

    - *Burns* v *Burns* [1984] Ch 317
    - *Gissing* v *Gissing* [1971] AC 886
    - *Pettitt* v *Pettitt* [1970] AC 777
    - *Midland Bank* v *Cooke* [1995] 4 All ER 562 (CA)

    Statute:

    - Matrimonial Proceedings and Property Act 1970, s37

2. **Failure of trust**

    If a settlor makes a declaration of trust which is ineffective because of, for example, uncertainty of objects, failure to satisfy formal requirements or perpetuity, then the trust property is held on resulting trusts for the settlor.

Key cases:
- *Barclays Bank* v *Quistclose Investments* [1970] AC 567
- *Re Gillingham Bus Disaster Fund* [1958] Ch 300
- *Grey* v *IRC* [1960] AC 1
- *Oughtred* v *IRC* [1960] AC 206
- *Vandervell* v *IRC* [1967] AC 291
- *Re Vandervell's Trusts (No 2)* [1974] Ch 269
- *Re West Sussex Constabulary Trust Fund* [1971] Ch 1
- *Re Trusts of the Abbott Fund* [1900] 2 Ch 326
- *Westdeutsche Landesbank Girozentrale* v *Islington BC* [1996] 2 All ER 961, HL (the speech of Lord Browne-Wilkinson casts doubt on the classification of resulting trusts made in *Re Vandervell's Trusts (No 2)* [1974], above).

3. **Surplus after performance**

In cases where there is a surplus a resulting trust in favour of the donor is usually inferred. As a matter of construction it is possible for the surplus to be either that of the trustees or beneficiaries absolutely.

Key cases:
- *Re Andrews's Trust* [1905] 2 Ch 48
- *Re Foord* [1922] 2 Ch 519
- *Re Trusts of the Abbott Fund,* above

4. **Voluntary transfer**
   - Realty: no presumption of a resulting trust
   - Personalty: opinion favours a resulting trust (no gift to the transferee)

Key cases:
- *Fowkes* v *Pascoe* (1875) 10 Ch App 343
- *Shephard* v *Cartwright* [1955] AC 431

- *Re Vinogradoff* [1935] WN 68
- *McGrath* v *Wallis* (1995) The Times 13 April

Sample Question

Joe organised holidays for school children. In 1992 he employed Harry, who was a travel agent, to book hotel accommodation for Joe's tours. In the course of doing this work, Harry contracted as principal with various hotels and paid accounts submitted by them for bookings made for Joe. Each month Joe paid Harry a fee for his services and also a sum equal to that which Harry owed the hotels for the accommodation booked for Joe's tours.

In 1994, Harry was in financial difficulties and Joe, who was worried about the danger to his business if Harry's business collapsed, proposed that he, Joe, pay a monthly sum into a special bank account at Harry's bank on which Harry could draw for the sole purpose of settling the invoices submitted by the hotels. Harry agreed to the arrangement and in May this year, Joe paid £50,000 into the special account to cover the hotel expenses incurred from January to April.

Harry has recently been declared bankrupt. Joe claims that the money in the special account ought to be applied to paying the debts owing to the hotels.

Advise Joe.

Further Reading

- HLT Textbook Chapter 6
- Pettit Chapter 8
- O'Hagan 'Indirect Contributions to Purchase of Home' (1993) 56 MLR 224
- Rickett 'Unincorporated Associations and their Dissolution' [1980] CLJ 88
- Thornton 'Illegality, Implied Trusts and the Presumption of Advancement' [1993] CLJ 394

See further Topic 5 on Constructive Trusts

TOPIC 5: Constructive Trusts

1. **Express informal agreement**

    Where there has at a time prior to acquisition or at some later date, been an agreement, arrangement or understanding reached between the parties that the property is to be shared beneficially. Party claiming beneficial interest must show that he or she has acted to his or her detriment or significantly altered his or her position in reliance on the agreement in order to give rise to a constructive trust or a proprietary estoppel.

    Key cases:

    - *Cooke* v *Head* [1972] 1 WLR 518
    - *Drake* v *Whipp* [1996] 1 FLR 826 (CA) (resulting trust principles excluded by express agreement as to ownership)
    - *Eves* v *Eves* [1975] 1 WLR 1338
    - *Lloyd's Bank* v *Rossett* [1990] 2 WLR 667
    - *Tinsley* v *Milligan* [1993] 3 WLR 126

2. **Direct financial contribution**

    In the absence of an express informal agreement, direct contributions to the purchase price will justify the necessary inference for the creation of a constructive trust.

    Key case:

    - *Lloyd's Bank* v *Rossett*, above, though contrast
    - *Midland Bank plc* v *Cooke* [1995] 4 All ER 562 (CA) (resulting trust concept used – see Topic 4)

3. **Breach of fiduciary duty**

    - Unauthorised remuneration
    - Unauthorised transactions on his own behalf
    - Purchase of property held in a fiduciary capacity
    - Sale of fiduciary's own property

Equity and Trusts 21

- Competition with a business he holds as fiduciary
- Confidential information acquired in capacity as fiduciary

Key cases:

- *Boardman* v *Phipps* [1967] 2 AC 46
- *Chase Manhattan Bank* v *Israel-British Bank (London) Ltd* [1981] Ch 105
- *Keech* v *Sandford* (1726) 2 Eq Cas 741
- *Industrial Development Consultants* v *Cooley* [1972] 1 WLR 443
- *A-G for Hong Kong* v *Reid* [1993] 3 WLR 1143

4. **Directors' remuneration**

   A director is barred from utilising any opportunity to profit from information received which is within the scope of his company's business.

   Key cases:

   - *Re Dover Coalfield* [1908] 1 Ch 65
   - *Re Gee* [1948] Ch 284
   - *Re Macadam* [1946] Ch 73

5. **Strangers to the trust**

   'Strangers' are persons who do not have duties in respect of the property apart from the constructive trust.

   a) 'Trusteeship de son tort'

   '... Where [a person], not being a trustee and not having authority from a trustee, takes upon himself to intermeddle with trust matters or to do acts characteristic of the office of trustee, he may thereby make himself what is called in law a trustee of his own wrong'

   Key case:

   - *Mara* v *Browne* [1896] 1 Ch 199

   b) 'Knowing assistance'

   Cases of 'knowing assistance' are concerned with situations

where the stranger has knowingly assisted in a dishonest and fraudulent design on the part of trustees. Four elements must be established:

- The existence of a trust
- The existence of a dishonest and fraudulent design
- The assistance by the stranger in that design
- The knowledge of the stranger

Key cases:

- *Agip (Africa) Ltd* v *Jackson* [1991] Ch 547
- *Baden* v *Société Générale* [1993] 1 WLR 509
- *Barnes* v *Addy* (1874) 9 Ch App 244
- *Brinks Ltd* v *Abu Saleh* (1995) The Times 23 October
- *Eagle Trust* v *SBC Securities* [1993] 1 WLR 489
- *Selangor United Rubber Estates* v *Craddock* [1968] 1 WLR 1555
- *Royal Brunei Airlines Sdn* v *Tan* [1995] 3 All ER 97
- *Westdeutsche Landesbank Girozentrale* v *Islington LBC* [1996] 2 All ER 961

c) Receiving/dealing

Knowing receipt or dealing may arise in three ways:

- Where the stranger knowingly receives trust property in breach of trust

    See the notes above, under knowing assistance, for the degree of knowledge necessary to hold a stranger a constructive trustee.

- Where the stranger receives trust property without notice of the trust but afterwards becomes aware of the trust and deals with it in a manner inconsistent with the terms of the trust
- Where the stranger receives trust property knowing it to be such without breach of trust and subsequently deals

Equity and Trusts

with the property in a manner inconsistent with the trusts

Key cases:

(As for knowing assistance, above)

d) Partners

Partners are in a fiduciary relationship with each other and any unauthorised benefits taken by one partner from the partnership assets will be held on a constructive trust.

Key cases:

- *Re Bell's Indenture* [1980] 1 WLR 1217
- *Mara* v *Browne*, above

6. Proprietary estoppel

In *Wilmott* v *Barber* (1880) 15 Ch D 96 Fry J considered that five elements had to be established before estoppel could operate:

- The plaintiff must have made a mistake as to his legal rights.
- The plaintiff must have done some act of reliance.
- The defendant, the possessor of a legal right, must know of the existence of his own right which is inconsistent with the right claimed by the plaintiff.
- The defendant must know of the plaintiff's mistaken belief of his rights.
- The defendant must have encouraged the plaintiff in his act of reliance.

Key cases:

- *Crabb* v *Arun DC* [1976] Ch 179
- *Re Basham* [1987] 1 All ER 405
- *Grant* v *Edwards* [1986] Ch 638
- *Jones* v *Jones* [1977] 1 WLR 438

Sample Question

In January 1987 April bought a run down freehold house called 'The Sewer' for £50,000. She paid for the purchase with £10,000 cash and a £40,000 mortgage with the Shredder Building Society.

In March 1987 she met Raphael and the couple soon became great friends. Raphael lived with his wife and three brothers who all disliked April.

In January 1988 April suggested to Raphael that he moved in with her as she was finding it difficult t meet all her monthly bills and that sharing such expenses would greatly help her. Raphael was reluctant to move away from his family as his father, Splinter, had told him that if he did move out to live with April, he would never be allowed back to live in the family home.

To settle Raphael's worries April assured him that if he did move in with her she would make sure that he would 'never have the need to return to his family home'. Reassured by this, Raphael moved in with April in February 1988.

April continued to pay the mortgage payments and Raphael paid for all the other household expenses. Raphael also carried out various repair jobs around the house and paid for new carpets throughout.

April and Raphael have recently split up and Raphael claims to be beneficially entitled to part of the house.

Advise April.

Further Reading

- HLT Textbook Chapter 7
- Pettit Chapter 9
- Allen 'Bribes and Constructive Trusts: *A-G for Hong Kong* v *Reid*' (1995) 58 MLR 87
- Berg 'Accessory Liability for Breach of Trust: *Royal Brunei Airlines v Tan*' (1996) 59 MLR 443
- Ferguson 'Constructive Trusts – A Note of Caution' (1993) 109 LQE 114
- Ferris 'The Advice of the Privy Council in *Royal Brunei Airlines* v *Tan*' (1996) 30 LTeach 111

- Hayton 'Constructive Trusts of Homes: A Bold Approach' (1993) 109 LQR 485
- Nolan 'From Knowing Assistance to Dishonest Facilitation: *Royal Brunei Airlines* v *Tan*' [1995] CLJ 505
- Oakley 'The Bribed Fiduciary as Constructive Trustee' [1994] CLJ 31
- Watts 'Bribes and Constructive Trusts' (1994) 110 LQR 178

TOPIC 6: Protective Trusts and Purpose Trusts – Trustees' Powers of Maintenance and Advancement

1. **Protective trusts**

    Protective trusts are designed to combine the advantages of a beneficiary having a fixed right to the income with those of discretionary trusts to prevent the property being dissipated. This can be done in two ways, expressly by the trust instrument or by taking advantage of the provisions of s33(1) Trustee Act 1925. The use of the s33(1) provisions is the most common way of creating a protective trust.

    a) Creation

    Section 33(1) provides a shorthand method of establishing a protective trust, where the settlor intends to settle any income including an annuity or other periodical payment, without setting out its terms in detail.

    b) Disentitling event

    So long as the protective trust runs in accordance with s33, a beneficiary will receive all the income arising from it as if he were a life tenant under a non-protective trust. But, should he attempt to do something which would deprive him of the right to receive some or all of the income in the future – an event within s33(1)(i), for example assigning his right to future income – the protective trust 'element' of the trust (under subs(i)) fails and is replaced by the second 'element' (under subs (ii)), a discretionary trust.

2. **Purpose trusts**

    A purpose trust is one not made for the benefit of human objects but for a particular purpose and, as a general rule, will be void for being a trust of imperfect obligation. An exception is a charitable trust: see Topic 7.

    a) Beneficiary principle

    Since a purpose trust has no human beneficiaries there is no-one who can demand performance in their favour.

Equity and Trusts

Key cases:

- *Re Astor* [1952] Ch 534
- *Morice* v *Bishop of Durham* (1805) 10 Ves 522

b) Exceptions

Three conditions would appear to be necessary before the court will uphold a purpose trust contrary to the general rule that it is void:

- The trust must be for a purpose which has been previously upheld by the court, eg the 'monument' and 'animal' cases
- The trust must be limited in perpetuity
- There must be someone who will execute the purpose trust

Key cases:

- *Re Dean* (1889) 41 Ch D 552
- *Re Endacott* [1960] Ch 232
- *Re Hetherington* [1989] 2 WLR 1094
- *Re Hooper* [1932] 1 Ch 38
- *Mussett* v *Bingle* (1876) WN 170
- *Pettingall* v *Pettingall* (1842) 11 LJ Ch 176
- *Re Thompson* [1934] Ch 342

c) Indirect beneficiaries

A gift to an unincorporated association would have as its indirect object a number of human beneficiaries. Poor drafting of the rule book of the association may result in such a gift being treated as a purpose trust.

Key cases:

- *Re Denley* [1969] 1 Ch 373
- *Re Lipinski* [1976] Ch 235

3. Maintenance

It is clear from s31(1) that when an infant beneficiary attains 18 the trustees must pay to him the income arising from his share of the trust property if the trust cannot be brought to an end at that time. But this provision does not authorise the trustees to pay to him income accumulated on his share during infancy. This is dealt with in s31(2).

4. Advancement

The purpose of the power is to permit trustees to advance capital to a beneficiary regardless of the type of interest which the beneficiary holds in the fund – no matter whether his interest is vested or contingent. The trustees can therefore give a beneficiary some of his entitlement before the time appointed, subject to the condition laid down in s32 TA 1925.

Key cases:

- *Re Pauling's Settlement Trusts* [1964] Ch 303
- *Pilkington* v *IRC* [1964] AC 612

Statute:

- Trustee Act 1925, s32

Sample Question

1. a) Discuss the proposition that there must be some identifiable person on whose application (to the court) a trust can be enforced in the context of:

    i) trusts for non-human objects; and

    ii) discretionary trusts.

   b) By his will a testator who died last year, after appointing Tug and Tow to be his executors and trustees, left £100,000 upon trust to invest the same and apply the income for a period of 20 years (i) as to one half thereof for the maintenance of the testator's horses and dogs, and (ii) as to the other one half for the benefit of such persons who had at any time during his lifetime been employed by him for a period of not less than one year and the children and remoter issue (whether born or to be born) of such employees in such shares as Tug and Tow shall from time to time think fit, and subject thereto to hold the capital and income upon trust for such person who shall, at the end of 20 year period, be Mayor of London.

Advise Tug and Tow.

2. Under the terms of a settlement, a personalty fund worth £150,000 is held by trustees upon trust for such of the settlor's grandchildren, Tom, Dick and Harriet, as attain the age of 15 in equal shares absolutely. Tom is now 25, Dick is 18 and Harriet is 13. Advise the trustees:

   a) whether they should now distribute one third of the capital of the trust to Tom;

   b) whether they should distribute any, and if so what, trust income and to whom;

   c) whether they may advance the sum of £25,000 out of capital to enable Dick to train for a commercial pilot's licence;

   d) whether they may pay out of trust moneys the school fees of Harriet who is about to go to boarding school.

3. By a settlement made in 1970, the settlor, Sam, directed the trustees, Tom and Terry 'to hold the income during the life of the settlor upon trust to pay or apply the same to or for the benefit of the settlor and of any wife whom he may marry and the children of the settlor ... or any of them as the trustees shall in their absolute discretion think fit'.

   'After the death of the settlor the trustees shall hold the income of the trust fund upon protective trusts for the benefit of any wife whom he may leave him surviving during her life.'

   a) On the assumption that Sam is unmarried aged 25, advise the trustees whether they may advance the sum of £10,000 to Sam to enable him to purchase a house in which he wants to practice his profession as a doctor, and whether they should comply with Sam's demand that all the income from the trust fund should be paid to him.

b) Advise the trustees as to the legal position on the assumption that Sam has just died, having married Mavis, and that Mavis was adjudicated bankrupt after his death.

Further Reading

- HLT Textbook Chapter 2, section 2.5; Chapter 9; Chapter 18, sections 18.8 and 18.9
- Pettit Chapters 3, 4 and 21

TOPIC 7:   Charitable Trusts

1. **Definition**
   There are three main requirements:
   - The trust must be of a charitable nature within the spirit and intendment of the preamble to the Statute of Elizabeth
   - It must promote a public benefit of a nature recognised by the courts as a public benefit
   - The purposes of the trust must be wholly and exclusively charitable

   Key cases:
   - *Commissioners of Income Tax* v *Pemsel* [1891] AC 531
   - *Scottish Burial Reform & Cremation Society* v *Glasgow Corp* [1968] AC 138

2. **Trusts of a charitable nature (public benefit)**

   a) Relief of the aged, impotent and poor
   - Relief

     Key case:
     - *IRC* v *Baddeley* [1955] AC 572
   - Aged

     Key case:
     - *Re Wall* (1889) 42 Ch D 510
   - Impotent

     Key cases:
     - *Re Lewis* [1955] Ch 104
   - Poverty

     Key cases:
     - *Dingle* v *Turner* [1972] AC 601 (public benefit)
     - *Re Coulthurst* [1951] Ch 661

- *Re Scarisbrick* [1951] Ch 622 (public benefit)
- *Re Gwyon* [1930] 1 Ch 255

b) **Advancement of education**
- Public benefit
  Key case:
  - *Caffoor* v *ITC* [1961] AC 584
- Aesthetic
  Key cases:
  - *Re Delius* [1957] Ch 299
  - *Re Pinion* [1965] Ch 85
- Research
  Key cases:
  - *Re Shaw* [1952] Ch 163
  - *Re Hopkins* [1965] Ch 669

c) **Advancement of religion**
- Advancement
  Key cases:
  - *Gilmour* v *Coates* [1949] AC 426 (public benefit)
  - *United Grand Lodge* v *Holborn BC* [1957] 1 WLR 1080
  - *Neville Estates* v *Madden* [1962] Ch 832 (public benefit)
  - *Re Watson* (1904) 49 SJ 54
- Office holders
  Key case:
  - *Dunne* v *Byrne* [1912] AC 407

d) Other purposes beneficial to the community, eg animals and recreational purposes
  Key cases:
  - *IRC* v *McMullen* [1981] AC 1 (sport)

- *IRC v Baddeley* [1955] AC 572 (public benefit)
- *Re Grove-Grady* [1929] 1 Ch 557
- *Re Wedgewood* [1915] 1 Ch 113
- *Guild v IRC* [1992] 2 WLR 397 (public benefit)

e) Politics

   Key case:
   - *McGovern v A-G* [1982] Ch 321

3. **Wholly and exclusively charitable**

   Each and every object or purpose designated must be of a charitable nature.

   Key cases:
   - *Blair v Duncan* [1902] AC 37
   - *Salisbury v Denton* (1857) 3 K and J 529

4. **Cy-près**

   a) General

   The usual presumption when a gift fails, and there is no provision in default, is that of a resulting trust in favour of the donor. However, in cases where the gift is for charitable purposes the doctrine of cy-près, or its alternatives, might be applied. In essence this ensures that in appropriate cases the gift is still applied for charitable purposes akin to the original objects for which it was given.

   b) Continuation of charitable purpose

   The date for deciding when the charitable purpose still exists is the date at which it is effectively dedicated to charity. This is important because if a gift has been given to charity it will forever, subject only to any express provisions of the donor, be used for charitable purposes.

   Key cases:
   - *Biscoe v Jackson* (1887) 35 Ch D 460
   - *Re Harwood* [1936] Ch 285

- *Re Jenkins* [1966] Ch 249
- *Re Rymer* [1895] 1 Ch 19
- *Re Satterthwaite* [1966] 1 WLR 277
- *Re Faraker* [1912] 2 Ch 488

5. **Corporate charities**

   There is no lapse if a gift is made to a named charity which has ceased to exist before the date the gift took effect but where its charitable work is nevertheless being carried on. In such cases it is really unnecessary to apply the cy-près doctrine because the charity is still in existence, albeit functioning under a different name.

   Key cases:
   - *Re Finger* [1972] Ch 286
   - *Re Vernon* [1972] Ch 300n

Sample Questions

1. Consider the validity and effect of the following provisions in a will:

   a) £50,000 to my friend, Harold, to be distributed by him amongst such of my friends (including himself) and in such shares as he sees fit;

   b) £50,000 to the Lord Mayor of London to be used in or towards the maintenance and support of the families of National Health Service workers in London whose actual net pay in a given week shall be less than £200;

   c) £100,000 to the vicar of the parish of St Swithen's to be used to purchase a site for a church hall. At the time of his death, a site for a church hall had already been purchased although a further £100,000 was required to build the hall;

   d) £20,000 to the headmaster of my old school, St Michael's, upon trust to invest the same during a period of 21 years to apply the income thereof in providing extra coaching for promising pupils at the school and subject thereto upon trust as to both capital and income for the vicar of St Swithen's.

2. Consider the validity of the following provisions in a will:
   a) £500,000 to my trustee upon trust to use the capital and income to establish a centre in England (i) for the formation of an informed international public opinion and (ii) for the promise of greater co-operation between the UK and other Commonwealth States in general.
   b) £750,000 to be invested and the income applied towards the relief of need suffered by employees and ex-employees of the National Coal Board as a result of strikes.
   c) £30,000 to my trustees upon trust to use the income for such period as the law allows for the maintenance of my pet tortoise, Emmy.
   d) The residue of my property upon trust for such charitable or benevolent purposes as my trustee may select.
3. a) In what major respects do charitable trusts enjoy special treatment and privileges as compared with non-charitable trusts?
   b) Consider the validity and effect of the following:
      i) a gift by will of £10,000 to the vicar of my parish church knowing that he will apply it for worthy and deserving objects;
      ii) a gift by cheque of £10,000 by an old student of Blanktown University in favour of the President of the Students' Union to be used to further the union's objects;
      iii) a gift of £20,000 cash sent to Bob Geldof 'to be applied for the relief of the starving and poor in East Africa'.

Further Reading
- HLT Textbook Chapters 10 and 11
- Pettit Chapters 13 and 14
- Fletcher 'Charities for the Advancement of Religion' (1996) 112 LQR 557
- Hopkins 'Trusts for the Advancement of Sport: The Recreational Charities Act 1958' [1992] CLJ 429

TOPIC 8: The Appointment, Retirement and Removal of Trustees

1. Appointment

a) The persons who may appoint a new trustee/s are set out in s36(1):

- The person/s nominated by the instrument, if any, creating the trust, or
- The surviving or continuing trustee/s, or the personal representatives of the last surviving or continuing trustee

Section 36(1) requires an appointment of a new trustee to be in writing

b) If no person in these categories is available to make the appointment, the court would appear to have the power to appoint in the last resort under s41 Trustee Act 1925 in the following instances:

- Where all the trustees named predeceased the testator
- Where the trustee was incapable of acting because of old age or some other infirmity such as mental illness
- Where there was doubt as to whether the statutory or an express power of appointment was exercisable
- Where the trustee was in enemy occupied territory

Statutes:

- Trustee Act 1925, s36, s40, s41
- Trusts of Land and Appointment of Trustees Act 1996, Pt II (effective from 1 January 1997): see summary, below

2. Removal of trustees

See generally above. The court has an inherent jurisdiction to remove a trustee and appoint a new one in his place or even remove him without appointing a replacement.

Statute:

- Trustee Act 1925, s36, s40, s41

3. **Termination – disclaimer, death, retirement**
    - A person appointed as a trustee is not obliged to take up the office and may disclaim it at any time before acceptance, however, there can be no disclaimer after acceptance
    - On the death of a trustee his trusteeship automatically terminates. On the death of a sole or last surviving trustee the trust estate devolves on his personal representatives
    - A trust may contain an express power permitting a trustee to retire. Apart from this, a trustee can retire when a new trustee is appointed in his place under s36(1). If no new trustee is to be appointed then he may retire under the provisions of s39(1).

    Key case:
    - *Re Tryon* (1844) 7 Beav 496

    Statutes:
    - Trustee Act 1925, s36
    - Trusts of Land and Appointment of Trustees Act 1996, Pt II – see summary, below

4. **Effects of the Trusts of Land and Appointment of Trustees Act 1996, P II: Summary**

    This Part of the Act applies to all trusts (whether of land or personalty) whenever created. Its aim is to give beneficiaries greater powers over the appointment of trustees.

    Background

    The pre-Act position was that trustees did not have to consult the beneficiaries when appointing new trustees: *Re Brockbank* [1948] Ch 206. Further, beneficiaries could not (except in the case of maladministration of the trust) force the trustees to retire.

    The aim of the new law is to provide an alternative to the only option formerly available to beneficiaries who wanted to control the appointment of trustees, namely to bring the trust to an end under the rule in *Saunders* v *Vautier* (1841) 4 Beav 115 and then reconstitute it with their own candidates as trustees (this option was unattractive from a tax perspective).

The Act establishes a new right for beneficiaries: s19. They can now give trustees a written direction to retire from the trust or to appoint a particular person as a trustee (ie the decision in *Re Brockbank* is reversed). This right can be exercised at any time (not just when the existing trustees have to make an appointment to augment their number).

However, there are a number of qualifying conditions to this right. The new right is only available if:

- there is no person who is given the power to appoint trustees in the trust instrument (this condition falls to be determined at the time when s19 is under construction);
- the beneficiaries are of full age and capacity; and
- it has not been expressly excluded by the trust instrument. The effect of the second condition (above) is to make Pt II inapplicable to discretionary trusts or where there are infant beneficiaries. The right can be excluded in respect of trusts created before the commencement of the Act.

Further, s19 takes effect subject to the restrictions imposed by the Trustee Act 1925 on the number of trustees: s19(5).

The effect of these provisions is clearly to pass more control to the beneficiaries. Further, the fact that Pt II applies both to trusts of land and trusts of personalty is in line with the Law Commission's goal of achieving greater parity (in this instance greater standardisation of beneficiaries' rights) between both types of trust. It is anticipated that many settlors or testators will want to exclude the operation of Pt II. Accordingly, it is most likely to apply in relation to a resulting or constructive trust (usually in respect of a family home) where the legal title is held by one person on trust for another who has contributed to the purchase price.

Sample Questions

1. a) In what circumstances and by whom may a trustee of a personalty settlement be removed from his trusteeship?

b) By his will a testator, who died last year, appointed Tick and Tock to be his executors and trustees, and left his residuary estate consisting of freeholds, leaseholds, shares in limited companies and bearer securities upon trust for his three sisters in equal shares absolutely. The three sisters are of full age and desire the trusts to continue.

Tock has been living in Spain for the last six weeks and although he intends to remain ordinarily resident in England, has indicated that he intends to spend quite a bit of time in Spain in the future. Tick wishes to appoint Little in place of Tock but the three sisters either want Tock to remain or Large to be appointed in his place. Advise Tick:

i) Who has the power to decide who is appointed?

ii) By whom the appointment will be made?

iii) By what method the appointment will be made?

iv) How the trust property will be vested in the new trustee?

2. a) What are the advantages, if any, of a new trustee being appointed by deed rather than simply by writing?

b) Consider the circumstances in which (i) administrative and (ii) discretions, exercisable by a trustee, may be delegated and the extent to which (if at all) the trustee so delegating will be liable for the delegate's acts and defaults.

c) In what circumstances (if any) will a trustee be liable for breaches of trust which occur after his retirement.

Further Reading

- HLT Textbook Chapter 12
- Pettit Chapter 15

TOPIC 9: Trustee Investment

1. **Common law duty**

    It is the duty of trustees seeking to argue that a particular investment falls within an express clause to prove that it actually does so.

    Key cases:
    - *Learoyd* v *Whitely* (1887) 12 App Cas 727
    - *Speight* v *Gaunt* (1883) 22 Ch D 727
    - *Nestlé* v *National Westminster Bank* [1993] 1 WLR 1260

2. **Trustee Investment Act investments**
    - Narrow range: Sch 1, Pts I and II Trustee Investments Act (TIA) 1961
    - Wider range: Sch 1, Pt II, TIA 1961

    Key case:
    - *Re Power* [1947] Ch 572

    Statutes and Orders:
    - TIA 1961, Sch 1
    - Charity Trustee Investments Act 1961 Order 1995 enables charitable trustees to invest up to 75% of their funds in wider-range investments
    - Trustee Investments (Division of Trust Fund) Order 1996 extends above relaxation of TIA 1961 to all trusts
    - Pensions Act 1995 ss35–36 will extend the investment powers of trustees of pension funds to an even greater degree when brought into force on 7 April 1997.

3. **Advice**

    a) Under s6(2) TIA 1961 the trustee is required when making Sch 1 Pt II and III and special range investments to 'obtain and consider proper advice on the question of whether the investment is satisfactory' having regard to:

- The need for diversification of investments of the trust fund, in so far as is appropriate to the circumstances of the trust: see s6(1)(a).
- The suitability of the trust of investments of the description proposed: see s6(1)(b).

Under s6(4) 'proper advice' for the purposes of s6(2) means 'the advice of a person who is reasonably believed by the trustee to be qualified by his ability in and practical experience of financial matters', such as a stockbroker or accountant.

b) Trustee investing in mortgages will be protected from breach of trust if:

- he acts on the report of a competent and independent surveyor or valuer, and
- the loan does not exceed two-thirds of that person's valuation, and
- the loan was made under the surveyor/valuer's advice

4. **Land**

   Under s73(1)(xi) Settled Land Act (SLA) 1925, it is provided that the purchase of freehold land or leasehold property of 60 years unexpired term at the time of purchase is an authorised investment for the purposes of the SLA. Section 28(1) Law of Property Act 1925 providesd that the trustees of a trust for sale have all the powers of the tenant for life and trustees of an SLA settlement, and it is specifically stated that they shall have the same powers of investment as apply under the SLA.

5. **Enlargement of investment powers**

   In *Trustees of the British Museum v A-G* [1984] 1 WLR 418 Megarry V-C suggested five guidelines to be considered when deciding what extended investment powers should be conferred:

   - The extent of provision for advice and control
   - Where very wide investment powers are being considered it would be appropriate to divide the trust fund so that a fraction of it is in safe or relatively safe investments.

- The combined effect of width, division, advice and control should be considered as they intereact.
- The size of the fund should be considered as greater risks may be justified with a larger fund.
- The object of the trust should be considered so that if it requires greater capital resources greater risks may be justified.

Key cases:
- *Re Kolb* [1962] 3 All ER 811
- *Trustees of the British Museum* v *A-G*, above

6. **Profits and losses**
    - Where a profit is made as a result of a breach of trust the beneficiaries are entitled to claim it as it is subject to the trusts.
    - Only if the profits and losses result from the same transaction or the same policy decision to adopt a particular course of action may a set-off be permitted.
    - Where a loss has occurred to the trust estate as a result of a breach by the trustee, he is liable to replace the loss with interest.

Key cases:
- *Bartlett* v *Barclays Bank* [1980] Ch 515
- *Dimes* v *Scott* (1827) 4 Russ 195

7. **General measure of liability**

    The measure of liability for a breach of trust generally is the loss, direct or indirect, caused to the trust estate.

    - If a trustee makes an unauthorised investment he will be liable for the loss incurred on realising it.
    - If a trustee improperly retains an unauthorised investment he will be liable for the difference between the price for which it is sold and that which would have been received if it had been sold at the proper time.

- If a trustee improperly sells authorised investments he must replace them or pay the difference between the price received and the cost of replacement.
- Trustees should meet a direction to invest within a reasonable time. Failure results in them being liable for interest lost if the property is not invested.

Key cases:
- *Knott* v *Cottee* (1852) 16 Beav 77
- *Jaffray* v *Marshall* [1993] 1 WLR 1285

8. Contribution and indemnity

a) Contribution

Since 1978 the Civil Liability (Contribution) Act has given the court power to award contributions in favour of one trustee against another on the basis of what it considers to be just and equitable having regard to the circumstances of the case. This right, or potential right, to a contribution does not arise if the trustee can alternatively claim an indemnity.

b) Indemnity

A trustee may be given an indemnity for the losses against his co-trustee as opposed to a mere contribution. Cases where an indemnity has been awarded are:

- Where the co-trustee was entirely to blame for the breach of trust or where the co-trustee got all the benefits of the breach
- If the active trustee was a solicitor whose advice or control was relied upon by the other trustees thereby causing them to participate in the breach of trust
- If the co-trustee was a beneficiary under the trust, then the breach may be made good out of his interest as far as possible before applying the contribution rules

Key cases:
- *Chillingworth* v *Chambers* [1896] 1 Ch 685

Statute:

- Civil Liability (Contribution) Act 1978

Sample Questions

1. a) In what circumstances, if any, may a trustee deviate from the terms of a trust?

   b) Under the terms of a settlement, X and Y were directed to hold certain government stock upon trust for A for life with remainders over. The settlement contains no special investment clause. At the instigation of A, X and Y were persuaded in the summer of 1987 to sell the government stock (then worth £50,000) and apply the proceeds in purchasing a work of art for £25,000 and invest the remaining £25,000 in unlisted securities.

   X and Y have recently sold the work of art for £40,000 and the unlisted securities for £10,000 (both these prices are full market values) and have reinvested the proceeds in government stock worth £50,000. Had they retained the original government stock it would now have been worth £55,000.

   Advise X and Y on the extent of their liability for breach of trust and of any right of recourse they may have.

2. Jacob and Daniel have been trustees of Philip's Trust deed since January 1996. In April 1996 Jacob, a stockbroker, suggested to Daniel, who has no knowledge or understanding of stocks and shares, that a sum of £100,000 in the trust fund should be invested in British Jingo plc. This was a recently formed British public company which had acquired the business of providing prison facilities to the Government in Britain. Jacob believes that since it was to be a monopoly business n this field, its future prospects were excellent and the dividends record likely to be very good. Daniel agreed to the suggestion.

   Jacob and Daniel also agreed to loan £20,000 on mortgage in respect of a shop in a slum district which was valued at £55,000.

   In December 1996 British Jingo plc go into liquidation.

Advise Jacob and Daniel as to the validity of the above investments, and their need to review investments of the trust fund.

3. Jane and Roger are trustees of the Jones' family trust. They are both strongly opposed to drinking and smoking and will not invest in any organisation that is connected with either activity. They are considering making the following investments:

   a) a mortgage of The Elms, a freehold property valued two years ago at £109,000. They are considering lending £90,000;

   b) shares in a public company;

   c) shares in a private company;

   d) Income bonds;

   e) a painting by a local artist whose work is becoming collectable.

   Advise Jane and Roger on the suitability of these investments.

Further Reading

- HLT Textbook Chapters 14 and 20
- Pettit Chapter 18

TOPIC 10: Variation of Trusts

1. **Inherent jurisdiction**

   The following are cases where the court could, under its inherent jurisdiction, give trustees additional powers to allow a variation in the terms of a trust:

   - Cases in which the court has effected changes in the nature of an infant's property. (This is now only of historical interest.)
   - Cases in which the court has allowed the trustees of settled property to enter into some business transaction which was not authorised by the settlement
   - Cases in which the court has allowed maintenance out of income which the settlor or testator directed to be accumulated
   - Cases in which the court has approved a compromise on behalf of infants and possible after-born beneficiaries

   Key cases:
   - *Chapman v Chapman* [1954] AC 429
   - *Hambro v Duke of Marlborough* [1994] 3 All ER 332

2. **Other provisions**

   - The effect of Trustee Act (TA) 1925, s53 is to empower the court to order property to be sold and conveyed so that the proceeds of sale may be used for the infant beneficiary's maintenance, education or benefit.
   - Trustee Act 1925, s57 extended the powers of the court so as to allow a variation in the terms of a trust other than in cases of emergency; a variation can be made here in cases of expediency.
   - Settled Land Act 1925, s64 is wider than s57 TA 1925 because, unlike s57, it is not limited to managerial or administrative acts but also allows alteration in the beneficial interests. This applies even if the beneficiaries

themselves are sui juris and strongly opposed to the proposed variation.
- Under the Mental Health Act 1983 the Court of Protection is given wide powers, extending to the power of settlement, in respect of the property of a patient who falls within its remit.

3. **Variation of Trusts Act 1958**

   a) General

   Section 1(1) Variation of Trusts Act 1958 gives the court a discretionary power to approve arrangements or variations on behalf of four classes of persons, namely:
   - Any person having, directly or indirectly, an interest, who by reason of infancy or other incapacity is incapable of assenting
   - Any person who may become entitled, directly or indirectly, to an interest under the trusts as being at a future date or on the happening of a future event
   - Any person unborn
   - Any person with a discretionary interest under protective trusts where the interest of the principal beneficiary has not failed or determined, any arrangement varying or revoking all or any of the trusts, or enlarging the powers of the trusts of managing or adminstering any of the trust property

   b) Variation or re-settlement?

   The scope of s1(1), although wide as to the nature of the arrangement that may be put before the court for approval, is narrow in its scope in that the court may only approve variation on behalf of the persons who fall within the provisions of s1(1)(a) to (d). A variation on behalf of any person who is not within the categories set out in s1(1) must have the consent of all such persons to the variation.

   c) Settlor's intention

   Before the court approves an 'arrangement' under the 1958 Act it must be satisfied that it is fair and proper in the light of the purpose of the trust as it appears from the trust instrument and any available evidence.

Key case:

- Re Steed [1960] Ch 407

d) Classes

Under s1(1)(b) the court may vary a trust on behalf of persons who might become entitled at a future date or future event as members of a class which is ascertainable only at a future time.

Key cases:

- Re Moncrieff [1962] 1 WLR 1344
- Re Suffert [1961] Ch 1

e) Benefit

Under s1(1) a variation may only be approved on behalf of any person falling with s1(1)(a) to (c) if it is for the 'benefit' of that person. 'Benefit' seems to be given a liberal interpretation, it is not confined to financial benefit but also includes moral or social benefit.

Key cases:

- Re Remnant [1970] Ch 560
- Re Seale [1961] Ch 574
- Re Tinker [1960] 1 WLR 1011
- Re Weston [1969] 1 Ch 223

Statute:

- Variation of Trusts Act 1958

Sample Questions

1. 'In general the court has no power to sanction a departure from the terms of a trust even though such a departure might well be advantageous for the beneficiaries.'

    Consider how far this statement is true having regard to (a) the statutory provisions; (b) general equitable jurisdiction.

2. Craig, who died recently, has two sisters, Jenny and Sarah. Craig left all his property upon trust to Jenny for life, then half to Jenny's children and grandchildren, and the other half to Sarah's children and grandchildren in remainder, provided they all remained orthodox Jews and lived in England.

   Jenny has two children, Emily aged 10 and Jason aged 19. Sarah has one child, Malcolm aged 17.

   Jenny, who is a widow, has recently met Patrick who is of the Roman Catholic faith. Jenny wishes to marry Patrick in a Roman Catholic Church and, therefore, has decided that she and her children must convert to Roman Catholicism. Also, Patrick has told Jenny that when they are married they should live in Southern Ireland because the proposed taxes in Ireland will be lower than the English taxes.

   Advise Jenny as to whether the trust can be altered to remove the religious and domicile restrictions from the trust.

Further Reading
- HLT Textbook Chapter 19
- Pettit Chapter 22

TOPIC 11: Breach of Trust: Defences

1. **Impounding a beneficiary's interest**

   The right to impound exists in equity and under TA 1925, s62. The right in equity arises in cases of concurrence or consent to breach if the beneficiary obtained a benefit from it, but is available regardless of benefit in cases of instigation of breach. The right to impound under s62 is wider than the equitable right in that it is not dependent on showing benefit to the beneficiary.

   Before the court will exercise its discretion under s62, it must be shown that the beneficiary knew that what he was instigating or requesting was a breach of trust.

   Key cases:

   - *Fletcher v Collis* [1905] 2 Ch 24
   - *Holder v Holder* [1968] Ch 353
   - *Re Pauling* [1964] Ch 303
   - *Re Somerset* [1894] 1 Ch 231

   Statute:

   - Trustee Act 1925, s62

2. **Trustee Act 1925, s61**

   Under TA 1925, s61 the court has jurisdiction to relieve trustees from liability for certain breaches of trust, if it appears that a trustee has acted honestly and reasonably, and ought fairly to be excused for the breach of trust.

   Key cases:

   - *Re Tollemache* [1903] 1 Ch 955
   - *Re Turner* [1897] 1 Ch 536
   - *Re Stuart* [1897] 2 Ch 583

3. **Limitation**

   The Limitation Act 1980 provides that, as a general rule, no action can be brought to recover trust property in respect of a breach of trust after six years from the date upon which the right of action accrued: see s21(3).

In two cases there is no limitation period according to s21(1)(a) and (b):

- In respect of any fraud or fraudulent breach of trust
- Recovery from the trustee of trust property or the proceeds thereof in his possession and converted to his use.

Sample Question

In what circumstances, if any, may a trustee rely on (1) lapse of time or (2) a claim to have acted reasonably and honestly, as a defence to an action for breach of trust?

Further Reading

- HLT Textbook Chapter 20
- Pettit Chapter 23
- Heydon 'Causal Relationships Between a Fiduciary's Default and the Principal's Loss' (1994) 110 LQR 328
- Nolan 'Targetting Trustees: Liability for Breach of Trust' [1994] CLJ 450

TOPIC 12: Breach of Trust: Proprietary Remedies

1. **Common law**

   Tracing at common law is concerned with protecting the immediate right to possession. The right to trace at common law may arise out of an immediate right to possession under a contract for bailment or hire-purchase, but cannot be classified as proprietary in the same sense as in equity.

2. **Equity**

   a) Fiduciary duty

   Tracing in equity is not possible unless there is an *initial* fiduciary relationship, which may arise from a resulting or constructive trust as well as an express trust.

   Key cases:
   - *Re Diplock* [1948] Ch 465
   - *Westdeutsche Landesbank Girozentrale* v *Islington LBC* [1996] 2 All ER 961 (HL)

   b) Property right

   If there is no property to trace then tracing will not help.

   Key case:
   - *Re Hallett* (1880) 13 Ch D 696

   c) Mixing of funds

   Tracing in equity is not defeated by mixing of funds.

   Key case:
   - *Re Hallett*, above

   d) Mixed with trustee's property

   This will normally occur when the trustee mixes the trust money with his own in an active banking account. It is for the trustee to prove what proportion of the mixed fund belongs to him, otherwise the whole will be treated as trust property.

Key cases:
- *Re Hallett*, above
- *Re Oatway* [1903] 2 Ch 356
- *Roscoe* v *Winder* [1915] 1 Ch 62

e) Mixed with another trust or innocent volunteer
- A trustee will be in breach of trust if he mixes the funds he holds in each of his fiduciary positions.
- If an innocent volunteer is given trust money by the trustee and he mixes it with his own money in, eg, his bank account, there will be a right to trace but it will be subject to the doctrine of notice.

Key cases:
- *Clayton's Case* (1816) 1 Mer 572
- *Re Diplock*, above
- *Sinclair* v *Brougham* [1914] AC 398 – overruled by HL in
- *Westdeutsche Landesbank Girozentrale* v *Islington LBC*, above

f) Limits to tracing

Tracing in equity will not be allowed if it will produce equitable results. For example,
- A bona fide purchaser for value of the legal estate without notice takes the property free from all equities.
- If the consequences of tracing are such that they would produce hardship or injustice to those against whom it is sought.

Key case:
- *Re Diplock*, above

Sample Questions

1. Flick is a trustee of two settlements, Settlement No 1 and Settlement No 2. In January of this year he received a cheque for £10,000 representing dividends from investments in

Settlement No 1 and paid it into his personal bank account which at the time had a credit balance of £5,000. In February he sold investments forming part of Settlement No 2 for £12,000 and paid this into the same account. In March he withdrew £15,000 from the account and bought shares in his own name in X Co Ltd. In April he won £10,000 on the pools and he paid this sum into the same account. In May he withdrew £12,000 from the account and gambled it away. He has now been adjudicated bankrupt. The shares in X Co Ltd are currently worth £30,000.

Advise the beneficiaries of each settlement as to their respective claims.

2. By a settlement made by Smith, the trustees, Dum and Dee, were directed to hold a trust fund consisting of shares and debentures in Alpha plc, a public limited company, and certain government stock, on trust to pay the income to Adam for life remainder to his children. The settlement contains no special investment clause except a provision that, before making any change of investment, the trustees should first obtain the consent in writing of Smith.

In 1992, Dum and Dee, with the consent in writing of Smith, sold the shares in Alpha to one of themselves, Dum, for £200,000 (their quoted value) and invested the proceeds in the purchase of shares in Beta plc, another public limited company.

In 1993, Dum and Dee, with the written consent of Smith, sold the government stock for £500,000 (its quoted value) and invested the proceeds in the purchase of freehold offices in Docklands.

In 1994, Dum and Dee, without the consent of Smith but with the encouragement of Adam, sold the debentures in Alpha plc for £100,000 (their market value) and invested the proceeds in shares of Delta plc, another public limited company.

The shares in Alpha plc are now worth £300,000; the shares in Beta plc are now worth £100,000; the shares in Delta plc are now worth £200,000 and the freehold offices are worth £250,000.

Advise:

a) Adam's children,

b) Dum and Dee jointly as trustees,

c) Dum individually,

as to their respective legal positions.

Further Reading

- HLT Textbook Chapter 21
- Pettit Chapter 24
- Andrews 'Tracing and Subrogation' [1996] CLJ 199
- Bryan 'The Meaning of Notice in Tracing Claims' (1993) 101 LQR 368
- Fennell 'Misdirected Funds and Remedies for Breach of Trust' (1994) 57 MLR 38
- Gardner 'Two Maxims of Equity' [1995] CLJ 60
- Rickett 'Equitable Compensation: the Giant Stirs' (1996) 112 LQR 27
- Tettenborn 'Trust Property and Conversion: An Equitable Confusion' [1996] CLJ 36